KEY
CURRICULUM
ENGLISH

One-A-Week 2
Comprehe

GW00601342

"Why Do We Dream ?"

Peter Howard

A COPIABLE RESOURCE

One-A-Week Comprehension Book 2 is the second of three books aimed at lower secondary pupils to improve their reading and vocabulary Students are presented with interesting study passage based on questions which may puzzle them.

Hopefully, students' general knowledge will increase as they work through the series.

Pupils are required to read and search for answers in the text. Questions involving a basic knowledge of grammar are introduced. The children also practise writing sentences correctly, and are asked to create their own sentences relevant to the text.

ISBN 1-90236-153-9

Contents

Why Does a Bee Sting?

Only rarely do bees attack anyone unless they have been provoked. As a rule, they sting only when people try to kill them or drive them away. Then they become alarmed and use, in self defence, the weapons that nature has given them.

The sting is really a fine, sharp, barbed tube through which a drop of poison can be injected. It is the worker bee that stings.

We often hear that a bee can only sting once and then it dies. What generally happens, is that a person who is stung, instantly knocks the offending bee away, tearing the sting from its body. This prevents the insect from withdrawing its sting naturally. The bee is so badly injured that it dies.

So, it is true to say that a bee can sting as often as we allow it, if we do not pull the stinger away from its body.

COPIABLE PAGE

Key Curriculum Publications Ltd.

1   Do bees often sting people?   _____

2   Is it possible for a bee to live after it has stung you?   _____

3   What kind of a bee stings?   A _____ bee

4   What does a bee inject when it stings?   _____

5   Which word means 'stirred up'?   _____

6   Which word means the opposite of 'allows'?   _____

7   Which word means 'pulling out'?   _____

8   Does the barb on a bee's tube point backwards?
(Use your dictionary if you do not know what a 'barb' is)   _____

9   Write the adverb in the opening sentence that tells
how often bees attack.   _____

10   The opening sentence consists of two parts.
Which word is the conjunction (joining word)?   _____

11   Use the words below to make a long sentence. The first four words make
the beginning of the sentence. Use a comma and add the conjunction 'but'.
Use the last four words to finish the sentence. Begin with the word written
with a capital letter.

> painfully   sting   Bees   sometimes   always
> honey   make   they

_____

_____

12   Write a sentence describing what a bee looks like. Use at least one adjective
as a colour.

_____

Can a Fly See All Ways At Once?

A fly cannot quite see in all directions at once because one part of each eye lies flat against its head. It cannot see directly behind. But it is true that a fly can see in many more ways or directions than we can.

This does not mean that a fly sees more clearly than we do. It has what we call a wider field of vision. This allows it to see much more without moving its eyes.

The main reason that a fly is able to do this is because it has two large eyes that take up most of the room in its head. Besides this, each eye is made up of about 4000 six-sided lenses. No two lenses are aimed in exactly the same direction, and each lens works on its own—no wonder it can see anything that moves all around it!

The fly is not alone in having many smaller eyes. Most insects and ants also have what we call 'compound eyes'.

Key Curriculum Publications Ltd.

Correction Text

Resources from corden92@btinternet.com

Extract from The Recruit by Robert Muchamore.
J

It was the first time james had been bak to primary skool since his last day as a puple before the sumer holidays. A few mums stud at the gate gnattering.

"wheres your mum, james" someone asked.

Off her face, james said sourly.

There was no way james was covering for her after shed kiked him out of the flat. he sore the other mums exchange glances.

"I want Medle of Honour for Playstation," one of them asked. "can she get it?"

jaes srugged, "coarse, half price, cash only/"

"will you rememember, James?"

No. give us a bit of paper with your name and fone no. and ill pas it on.

The gaggle of mums started joting things down. Trainers, jewelery, radio-controled car. James stuft the papers into his school blazer.

"I need it buy Tuesday," someone said.

James wasnt in the mood.

"if you want to tell my mum sumthing, write it down. I wount rember.

James	James 3x	shrugged
back	she'd	
school	kicked	
pupil	He	
summer	saw	
took	medal	
attering	Can	
here's	James	

Correction Text

Resources from corden92@btinternet.com

Extract from The Recruit by Robert Muchamore.

E _Answers_

His mum was nowhere near as fat in those days. Her face woould appeare in the end of the tunnele with a daft grin. She'd speak in a deep voisce, _I'm coming to eat you up, jJames._ It was cool, because the tunnele had a killer echo when you were sitting inside. James tryied the eceho:

"I'm a total idiot".

The eceho agreed with him. He pulled his coat huood up and did the zip to the top so it covered half his fasce.

After half an hour sulking, jJames knew he had 2two options: stay in the tunnele for the rest of his life, or go home and get killed.

James stepped into the hallway of his flat and cheqcked the mobile fphone on the table under the coat rack:

12 MISSED CALLS

UNIDENTIFIED NUMBER

It looked lyike skchool had been trying to get hold of his mum pretty bad, but she hadn't answered. jJames thanked god, but wuondered why she hadun't pickedt up. Then he notisced uUncle rRon's jacket hanging up.

Uncle Ron had turned up when jJames wasoz a toddler. It was like having a loeud, smelly runng in the flat. Ron smoked, drank and only went out to go to the pub. He got a job wonsce, but it only lasted a fortnighte.

Correction Text

Resources from corden92@btinternet.com

Extract from The Recruit by Robert Muchamore.

G

"mum, sumthink happened at skool. It was an accident"

"wet your pants again, did you" ron gigled.

James didnt want to take the bait.

"listen, james, me darlin'," gwen said, sluring her words.

Wwhatever trouble youre in this time well talk later. go and get your sisten from skool. Ive had a few to many drinkies and Id better not drive."

"im sorry, mum, its really searius. I have too tel you ..."

"just get youre sister, james," his mum said sturnly "My head is pounding.

"laurens big enof to cum home on her own," james said.

She isn't, ron interupted. "Do what your told. He needs my boot up is backside if you ask me.

"How much money dos he wont this time james asked sarcasticly.

Gwen waved her hand in frunt of her face. She was fed up with both of them.

Correction Text

Extract from The Recruit by Robert Muchamore.

B Answers

James' mum was huge. She had to order her clothes out of a special catalogue for fat people. It was a nightmare being seen with her. People pointed, stared. Little kids mimicked the way she walked. James loved his mum, but he tried to find excuses when she wanted to go somewhere with him.

"I went for a five-mile jog yesterday," Samantha said. "two laps around James' mum."

James looked up from his exercise book.

"That's so funny, Samantha. Even funnier than the first three times you said it."

James was one of the toughest kids in Year Seven. Any boy cussing his mum would get a punch. But what could you do when it was a girl?

Next lesson he'd sit as far from Samantha as he could.

"Your mum is so fat –"

James was sick of it. He jumped up. His stool tipped over backwards. What is it with you, Samantha?" James shouted.

The lab went quiet. Every eye turned to the action.

"What's the matter, James?" Samantha grinned. "Can't take a joke?"

1   Do planets burn in the sky?   _____

2   Is the Sun a planet or a star?   a _____

3   What two planets are mentioned in the story?   _____

4   Which is larger, a planet or a star?   a _____

5   Which word means 'shines back'?   _____

6   Which word means 'goes around'?   _____

7   Which word means 'far away'?   _____

8   Circle the word which means the same as 'unwavering'.

     moving   flickering   steady   unwise

9   Write the adjective in the opening sentence that tells what sort of body.   _____

10   In the first sentence of the second paragraph there is an adverb telling how. Write this adverb.   _____

11   Use these words to make a sentence. Underline the adjective. Begin with the proper noun.

     star   the   Venus   in   looks   sky   like

     a   bright

_____

_____

12   Write a sentence telling the difference between a star and a planet.

_____

_____

Do planets burn in the sky? _____

Is the Sun a planet or a star? a _____

What two planets are mentioned in the story? _____

Which is larger, a planet or a star? a _____

Which word means 'shines back'? _____

Which word means 'goes around'? _____

Which word means 'far away'? _____

Circle the word which means the same as 'unwavering'.

moving   flickering   steady   unwise

Write the adjective in the opening sentence that
tells what sort of body. _____

In the first sentence of the second paragraph there
is an adverb telling how. Write this adverb. _____

Use these words to make a sentence. Underline the adjective. Begin with the
proper noun.

star   the   Venus   in   looks   sky   like

a   bright

_____

_____

Write a sentence telling the difference between a star and a planet.

_____

_____

1   Is there a spot where a fly cannot see?   _____

2   Does a fly need to move its eyes like we do?   _____

3   How many sides has each lens in a fly's eye?   _____

4   What name is given to creatures other than
    ants that have many eyes?   _____

5   Look up the word 'fly' in a dictionary.
    How many wings has it?   _____

6   Which word means 'the power of seeing'?   _____

7   Which word means the opposite of 'larger'?   _____

8   Which word means 'made of two or more parts'?   _____

9   Write the conjunction in the opening sentence that
    joins the two parts.   _____

10 Write the two adverbs in the second sentence that tells how it cannot see.

    _____   _____

11 Write the last sentence of the story again. Take out the words 'also', 'what',
    'we', 'call'. Use the word 'large' or 'small' before 'compound'. Only one of
    these words is correct.

    _____

    _____

12 Write a sentence telling why a fly can see so well.

    _____

    _____

Why Does Furniture Make a Noise at Night?

Have you heard furniture making a cracking or creaking sound at night?

Perhaps it may make similar sounds during the day, but there are so many other noises that we may not hear furniture cracking. Besides, at night, when everything is still, our hearing is more acute than usual.

The reason furniture cracks is because the wood either becomes smaller or larger. This happens when the temperature changes. After a hot day, for example, when parts of a chair have expanded, the wood contracts as the night becomes cooler. This causes noises as the wood or the joints change in shape.

The roof area of many houses is made of tiles or slates laid on a wooden frame. The wooden frame itself changes shape like the furniture. So if you hear a cracking noise in your roof, it is not a burglar, but the shrinking or expanding timbers.

Key Curriculum Publications Ltd.

1 Is it possible for the furniture to make a noise during the day? _____

2 Does wood make a noise because it gets old? _____

3 Besides a cracking noise, what other kinds of noise does furniture make? _____

4 What part of a roof is made of wood? _____

5 Which word means 'the same as'? _____

6 Does the word 'contracts' mean to grow smaller or grow larger? grow _____

7 Which word means the opposite of 'warmer'? _____

8 Circle the word which could have been used instead of burglar.

butler   gangster   visitor   house-breaker   gardener

9 Write whether the opening sentence is a statement, question or command. _____

10 Study the last sentence of the story. The two verbs ('hear' and 'is') are in the present tense or time. Change them both to past tense or time—as if it happened yesterday.

_____   _____

11 Use these words to make a question. Make the last word 'night'.

heard   your   night   at   creaking   you   house   have   in

_____

_____

12 Answer the question with Yes, or No, and two or three words.

_____

Is Your Body Wearing Away?

Almost every part of your body wears away, but no part disappears. The reason is that as parts wear away, they are replaced. Your second set of teeth wear away very slowly because your body does not replace teeth. Of course, if you do not look after them, they may decay quickly and be lost forever.

If you wore a pair of gloves every day, you would soon wear holes at the tips where your fingers fit. In the same way, without gloves, your finger wears away. But new cells are made all the time, and fresh skin grows to make your finger like new again. Your skin can be cut as many times as you like, but it still keeps healing by growing again.

Cells for making new bone are held in reserve in every bone in your body. They do nothing if things go well, but if a bone is broken, these cells spring into action. The doctor puts the broken ends together and leaves them. These bone cells, working in darkness, knit the broken ends together. The bone never breaks again at the same place because the cells have made the bone stronger still where the break occurred.

 Key Curriculum Publications Ltd.

1 Does every single part of your body wear away? _____

2 Is a worn second tooth replaced? _____

3 Do skin cells replace parts of fingers worn away? _____

4 What kind of cells would repair a broken thumb? _____

5 Which word means 'rot'? _____

6 Which word means the opposite of 'stale' or 'old'? _____

7 Which word means 'making well or whole'? _____

8 Which word means 'with little or no light'? _____

9 Write the adverb in the last sentence that tells
   more about the verb 'breaks'. _____

10 The opening sentence consists of two parts.
   Which word is the conjunction (joining word)? _____

11 Proofread this sentence which has three mistakes. Write it correctly below.

   I saw helen brake her arm when she felled.

   _____

   _____

12 Write a sentence telling how part of your body healed. Make the sentence a
   long one with a conjunction.

   _____

   _____

How Can We Tell a Star from a Planet?

A star is a glowing body like the Sun. It produces its own heat and light. A planet is not burning, but only reflects light from the Sun or star round which it orbits. The Earth is a planet that revolves round our own particular star, the Sun.

In the sky at night we see many twinkling stars that are shining brightly. Among them are planets that also shine, but they are reflecting light from the Sun. They are really very small bodies when compared to the Sun or any of the other stars. Yet some of the planets make a fine show in the sky, and the little Venus often looks larger than the real stars. That is because, although small, it is much closer to us, and looks big compared to the distant stars. In much the same way, your finger looks large if you hold it in front of your eyes when looking at a mountain far away.

How can we easily tell which are stars or which are planets when we look at the sky? The answer is that planets shine with a steady, unwavering light, whereas the stars seem to twinkle.

Key Curriculum Publications Ltd.

1 Do planets burn in the sky? _____

2 Is the Sun a planet or a star? a _____

3 What two planets are mentioned in the story? _____

4 Which is larger, a planet or a star? a _____

5 Which word means 'shines back'? _____

6 Which word means 'goes around'? _____

7 Which word means 'far away'? _____

8 Circle the word which means the same as 'unwavering'.

moving   flickering   steady   unwise

9 Write the adjective in the opening sentence that
tells what sort of body. _____

10 In the first sentence of the second paragraph there
is an adverb telling how. Write this adverb. _____

11 Use these words to make a sentence. Underline the adjective. Begin with the
proper noun.

star   the   Venus   in   looks   sky   like

a   bright

_____

_____

12 Write a sentence telling the difference between a star and a planet.

_____

_____

How Deep Is the Sea?

The sea varies in depth in the same way as the land varies in height. There are slopes descending gradually from the shore that become deeper and deeper. There are plains and tablelands that run for many kilometres at the same depth. There are precipices with sheer descents into chasms ten kilometres deep.

All these facts are known as a result of thousands of soundings taken over many years. Maps showing the depths of the oceans have been drawn. There are over 6000 spots where the depth is well over two kilometres deep.

The deepest sounding that has been made is 11 033 metres off the island of Guam. Soundings were once made by dropping a lead sinker attached to fine wire to the bottom of the sea. Today an apparatus is used that directs supersonic sound waves to the ocean bed. The interval between sending and receiving the reflected signals gives the depth of water.

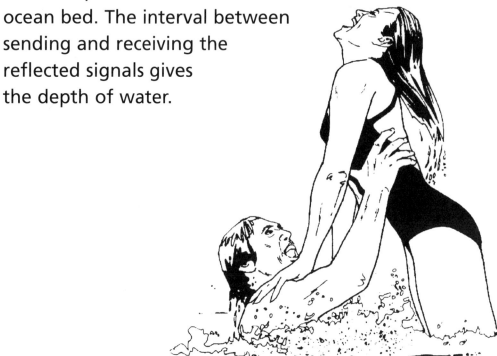

Key Curriculum Publications Ltd.

1   Is the bottom of the sea shaped like the land?   _____

2   To find the depth in the ocean today, is a
    lead weight used?   _____

3   Off which island is it very deep?   _____

4   What name is given to a deep hole below the sea?   _____

5   What is the verb used in the first sentence that
    means 'changes or alters'?   _____

6   Which word means 'a set of instruments'?   _____

7   Which word means 'faster than sound'?   _____

8   Circle the synonym (word that means the same)
    of the word 'interval' in the last paragraph.

        narrow   entrance   start   time

9   In the first sentence of the last paragraph there is an
    adjective that is formed from the word 'deep'.
    What is the noun that it tells more about?   _____

10 Write the proper noun from the story.   _____

11 Proofread the sentence below which has four mistakes. Write it correctly.

        Guam lays to the East of the phillipine islands.

    _____

    _____

12 Write a sentence about a scene of the sea bed that you have watched on
    television.

    _____

Why Does a Boomerang Come Back?

There are various kinds of boomerangs—heavy ones for fighting at close quarters, and lighter ones for throwing at birds or animals. One kind travels straight at first, but it is so shaped that air resists one part of it more than the other. It travels upwards and then in a curved path after its speed has slowed down and more or less comes back to the thrower. This kind can travel a distance of almost 100 metres before returning.

The ones that come right back to the thrower after making one or two circles are often called 'play boomerangs'. The Australian Aborigines practise throwing these to show their skill. Such boomerangs consist of a flattened, curved blade, usually quite flat on one side and slightly convex on the other. The weapon is slightly twisted and so always flies in a circle. It returns because its shape allows the air to keep it permanently in a turning position. An aeroplane with its rudder and certain controls jammed would also keep flying in a circle.

COPIABLE PAGE Key Curriculum Publications Ltd.

1 Was a light boomerang used by Aborigines for fighting? _____

2 Are the two blades of a boomerang exactly the same? _____

3 What are the boomerangs called that
   only travel in a circle? _____ boomerangs

4 What else besides a boomerang could keep flying
   in a circle? _____

5 Which word in the first paragraph means 'acts against'? _____

6 Besides 'twisted', which word means the
   opposite of 'straight'? _____

7 Which word means 'lasting a long time'? _____

8 Does the word 'convex' mean curved outwards or
   curved inwards? (Use your dictionary) _____

9 Write the phrase in the last sentence that tells how the plane is flying.

   _____

10 Write the adjective and proper noun that form the name of a race of people
   in the story.

   _____   _____

11 Write the last sentence of the first paragraph. Begin with 'A boomerang' instead
   of 'This kind'. Use words instead of the number 100.

   _____

12 Describe a boomerang for someone who has never seen one.

   _____

Will All Sharks Attack People?

You have probably seen pictures on television of the Great White shark. It has huge teeth and has been known to kill many people. Divers who search for shellfish have to always be on the lookout for this hungry shark.

But not all sharks attack people. Out of some 250 different kinds of sharks, only about a tenth of these are dangerous. The Port Jackson shark found off Australia, America and Japan is harmless. Its teeth are only made for crushing shells that it scoops up from the sea bed.

Another larger shark which grows to a length of 12 metres is also harmless. It is the Basking shark, which lives on minute plant life called plankton. Even larger is the harmless Whale shark. It too only feeds on plankton.

Even though most sharks will leave you alone, you must take care when swimming where the sea is warm. Always swim between the flags at a beach because lifesavers are watching for sharks. Never swim in the sea at night.

FRIEND?

COPIABLE PAGE   Key Curriculum Publications Ltd.

1 Do divers worry about Great White sharks? _____

2 Does the Port Jackson shark attack people? _____

3 What does the Basking shark eat? _____

4 Who watches for sharks on beaches that
   are marked with flags? _____

5 Which word means the same as 'look'? _____

6 Which word means 'one out of ten'? _____

7 Which word means 'very small'? _____

8 Which word means 'pressing together'? _____

9 Write the adjective used to describe the teeth
   of the Great White shark. _____

10 Write the three proper nouns which are names of countries.

_____ _____ _____

11 Write a sentence with these words. Start with the word beginning with a
   capital letter. End with the word 'beach'. Underline the adverb.

   between   the   can   swim   flags   at
   safely   beach   You

   _____

   _____

12 Write a sentence about a shark you have seen. Give the sentence two parts
   joined by 'which'.

   _____

   _____

How Do Fish Live in a Frozen Pond?

Have you noticed that ice cubes in a drink float on top? Ice is lighter than water so it does not sink. What we call a frozen pond, has a layer of ice floating on the top. It is not all solid ice, otherwise fish would be stuck and not be able to move. The fish quite happily swim below the ice, and being cold-blooded, do not really mind if the water becomes cold.

The problem for fish in a frozen pond then, is not the coldness of the water but the lack of oxygen. When a pond is not frozen, oxygen from the air above is passing into the surface of the water. The fish are taking oxygen from the water, but it is being replenished.

When a pond is frozen, this process is very nearly stopped. There may be gaps along the edge of the pond, but the best hope for fish to stay alive is for fresh water to enter from below the ice. If there is no fresh water coming in, then the fish may die unless the ice on the pond melts.

Key Curriculum Publications Ltd.

1   Does an ice cube sink to the bottom in a glass of water?   _____

2   Do fish worry about water that is cold?   _____

3   In a pond that is not frozen, what passes
    from the air into the water?   _____

4   What word is used to describe a pond that has
    a layer of ice over it?   _____

5   Which word tells us that fish do not have warm
    blood like we do?   _____

6   Which word means 'the outside of something'?   _____

7   Which word means 'a series of actions or
    changes that are taking place'?   _____

8   Which word means 'supplied or filled again'?   _____

9   In the first sentence there are two phrases. Write the phrase that tells more
    about the ice cubes. It is an adjectival phrase.

    _____

10 From the same sentence, write the phrase that tells where they float. It is an
    adverbial phrase.

    _____

11 Answer the question in the first sentence. Begin with 'Yes', (put a comma after
    this word). Then continue with 'I have' followed by the rest of the words.

    _____

    _____

12 Write a short sentence telling why an ice cube floats on water.

    _____

Why Do People Walk in Their Sleep?

There are two parts of the brain that control the way we move or act. One part has to do with all things we know we are doing. The other part has to with things that we do not realise we are doing—that is, we do without thinking.

We do many things without having to think. For instance, we breathe without thinking, and our heart beats without our thinking. Then there are things their learn to do and then do so well that we need not think about but do automatically, such as walking.

A person who walks in his or her sleep does so without thinking. He or she usually just gets out of bed and stands up. Sometimes the person walks a little way.

Sleepwalking occurs more with children than adults, and particularly those who have worries or problems. It does no harm to gently wake someone who is sleepwalking, because there is always a danger that he or she may have an accident. After being awakened, the sleepwalker will not remember having stepped out of bed.

Key Curriculum Publications Ltd.

1   Do we need to think when we want to breathe?   _no_

2   Do old people sleepwalk more than young people?   _no_

3   Do sleepwalkers usually walk a long or short way?   _short_

4   What danger does a sleepwalker face?   an _accident_

5   Which word in the first paragraph means the same
    as 'govern or regulate'?   _control_

6   Which word means 'grown-up people'?   _adults_

7   Which word means 'happens'?   _occurs_

8   Write the two words which both
    mean 'concerns' or 'anxieties'.   _____   _____

9   Write the adverbial phrase in the last sentence which tells where the
    sleepwalker stepped.

    _____

10 From the same sentence write the two common nouns.

    _____   _____

11 There are two parts to the first sentence. The joining word is 'that'. Write
    the first part alone. It should make sense.

    _____

12 Write a long sentence telling what you would do if you saw your brother,
    sister or a cousin sleepwalking.

    _____

    _____

What Makes the Wind Whistle?

Wind is air that moves across the Earth's surface. It can blow gently or fiercely. But the wind, or current of air, does not make a sound by itself. You may feel a draught, or a gust of wind, but you cannot hear it.

What you do hear, however, is the vibration, trembling or whistling that the wind makes when it forces itself through chinks of doors, windows or even down the chimney. It sets things vibrating that get in the way and this causes you to hear sounds which can even be quite musical at times.

Have you been frightened by noises in the house that the wind made? Well, if you went outside, that same wind would probably not have been at all frightening. It might have made a whistling or swishing noise as it passed through trees, but it should not have startled you.

The only time wind can be frightening is during a hurricane. Then the wind is very strong. It is the damage to property—especially roofs or houses—that causes harm.

Key Curriculum Publications Ltd.

1   Does the wind whistle through openings? _____

2   Does the wind make a noise in the sky? _____

3   Which word tells us the wind can blow softly? _____

4   What kind of wind can wreck things? _____

5   Which word means 'shivering' or 'quivering'? _____

6   Which word means 'a current of air in an enclosed space'? _____

7   Which word means 'cracks' or 'openings'? _____

8   Which word means 'people's possessions'? _____

9   The pronoun 'it' in the second sentence stands for a noun in the first sentence. Write the noun. _____

10 Look at the first sentence in the last paragraph. Write the adverbial phrase that tells when the wind can be frightening.

_____

11 Use the words below to write a sentence. Underline the pronoun. Begin with the word written with a capital letter.

wind   needs   it   yacht   A   the   to   move   make

_____

12 Write a long sentence telling about the time you were frightened by a noise caused by wind.

_____

_____

What Is a Skyscraper?

Many years ago, a skyscraper was a triangular sail which sailors spread above their ordinary sails. It was used when they were in calm seas. They hoped to catch a slight breeze to make their ship move. Nowadays the word is used to describe the gigantic buildings in some cities of the world.

The first skyscrapers were built in New York City. Land there cost a lot of money, so it paid to make office buildings tall. The first really giant skyscraper was the Empire State Building which is 381 metres tall with 102 floors. The building is almost a city of its own with 20 000 workers using its offices. The foundations are deep down in the rock beneath New York.

Taller skyscrapers have since been built. The Sears Tower in Chicago is 443 metres high with 110 floors. Most large cities have skyscrapers but they are not as tall. Most of them have more than 45 floors but less than 72 floors. However, architects think that it will be possible to build a skyscraper as high as 600 metres. Of course, like other skyscrapers, it will have to be built on solid foundations.

Key Curriculum Publications Ltd.

1 Who used the word 'skyscraper' long ago?   _____

2 Was land expensive in New York?   _____

3 Would the Empire State Building be twice as tall
   as Sydney's highest skyscraper?   _____

4 What are people called who design buildings?   _____

5 Which two words mean 'really large'? _____ _____

6 Which word means the opposite of 'rough'?   _____

7 Which word means 'the parts on which a
   building rests or stands'?   _____

8 Which word means 'to give a picture of'?   _____

9 Write the adjective in the first sentence that tells
   what shape something is.   _____

10 In the first sentence of the last paragraph an adjective is used that
   compares. Write this same adjective in its ordinary form.

   _____

11 The second sentence has two parts joined by 'when'. Write the sentence
   again by putting the joining word at the beginning.

   _____

   _____

12 Write a long sentence describing the tallest building you have seen. Use the
   joining words 'and', 'which'.

   _____

   _____

What Happens when Water Boils?

Water can be solid, liquid or gas, depending on its temperature. When water is very cold, at a temperature of 0 degrees Celsius, it becomes ice or solid. When heated to 100 degrees Celsius in its liquid form, it turns into steam or gas.

When we boil water in a saucepan, little bubbles of gas form in the water and rise to the top. After a while there will be no more water left if the heat is continually applied. The water will have all turned to steam or gas and gone into the air in the room.

Water that is turned to gas can only remain in that state if the temperature is hot enough. Hold a cold plate over a boiling saucepan and you will find that the plate has become wet. The warm steam or gas has suddenly cooled when striking the plate and has turned back into water.

Although you cannot see water in the air of a room, it is there. Take a glass of water and add a few ice cubes. This will make the sides of the glass cold. Any air that touches the sides of the glass will be cooled. The water in the air will be deposited on the sides of the glass. Run your finger along the outside of the glass and you will see that it is wet.

 Key Curriculum Publications Ltd.

1   At 50 degrees Celsius is water liquid or solid?   _____

2   Will water keep on boiling forever if a saucepan
    is left on a hot stove?   _____

3   Does cold or hot air hold water best?   _____ air

4   Circle the form water is in the air of your bedroom.

            gas   liquid   solid

5   Which word means 'constantly'?   _____

6   Which word means 'put or laid down'?   _____

7   Which word means the same as 'contacts'?   _____

8   Use your dictionary to find what country
    Anders Celsius was from.   _____

9   Which adverb in the second sentence tells how
    cold water is at 0 degrees?   _____

10 In the second part of the last sentence there is a word that is used instead
    of 'glass'. This is a pronoun. Write it.

    _____

11 Write the first sentence of the last paragraph. Move the joining word
    'Although' (conjunction) into the middle.

    _____

    _____

12 Write a sentence telling where you have seen water in the air deposited on
    something other than a glass of cold water.

    _____

What is Smoke Made of?

Smoke results from imperfect burning. Most things that are burnt would give off little or no smoke if they were burnt properly. There would be nothing left but gases, which we could not see, and which would very soon fly away.

When we light a fire to burn wood or rubbish, specks of unburnt material rise with the warm air created by the fire. This is smoke. Coal was once used by people for fires in their homes. Specks of unburnt coal and oily material carried up chimneys made a thick smoke that used to settle everywhere. Houses and buildings, especially in England, were blackened over the years. Now, in many places, coal is not allowed to be burned.

Many of our power stations still burn coal. Air is blown onto the fires so that they are kept very hot, and only a little smoke is formed. But there is still a lot of smoke around our large cities from open fires. This, together with smoke or exhaust from the burning petrol in cars, all make the air we breathe polluted.

Electric heating causes no pollution in the cities and perhaps soon there will be many electric cars which do not put fumes into the atmosphere.

1 Do some things burn perfectly? _____

2 What material was burnt that blackened
buildings in England? _____

3 What type of heating has no smoke? _____

4 Is some smoke caused by power stations? _____

5 What two words are used for smoke that comes from a car?

_____   _____

6 Which word means 'a state of something
being dirty or impure'? _____

7 One word tells us that smoke is caused by burning
that is not complete. Write it. _____

8 Which word means 'very small parts'? _____

9 Write the two proper nouns in the story.

_____   _____

10 In the last paragraph, the sentence has three parts. Write the two joining
words.

_____   _____

11 The second sentence has two parts joined by 'if'. Write the sentence again by
putting the joining word at the beginning, followed by 'most things were
burnt properly'. You can leave out three words—'are', 'that' and 'burnt'.

_____

_____

12 Write a sentence describing smoke you have seen from a fire.

_____

Water, like everything else, is pulled towards the Earth's core by gravity. When you spill water on the floor, all parts of it therefore try to flow as near as possible to the centre of the Earth. The surface then becomes level. Even a rubber ball, if it was melted, would spread out in the same way as water and become level.

However, if we think about our Earth's shape, we know that water on the floor is not exactly level but must follow the curve of the earth. Water in the smallest pool or basin must follow this law, but, of course, the curve is so slight that we cannot see it.

On the other hand, the curve on water in a huge lake or ocean can be seen. Ships travelling away in the distance gradually disappear over the edge of the curve at the horizon. Ships coming over the horizon gradually rise up as they approach. So the real answer to this question is that surface water is always curved in one way — the way in which the Earth itself is curved.

 Key Curriculum Publications Ltd.

1 Does gravity pull water downwards? _____

2 Is all water on seas perfectly level? _____

3 Is the surface of the Earth curved or flat? _____

4 What objects in the story disappear or appear
   over the horizon? _____

5 Which word means 'middle part'? _____

6 Which word means 'made into a liquid'? _____

7 Which word means 'a set of rules'? _____

8 Write the word used for 'draw nearer'. _____

9 Write the adjective in the story which tells what
   kind of ball. _____

10 In the last paragraph, there is an adverb that tells
   how ships rise up or disappear. Write it. _____

11 Complete this sentence to explain how a carpenter's level works. Use the
   words below.

        finds   a   level   its   liquid   own   always

   A carpenter's level works because _____

   _____

12 Write a long sentence telling why a ship disappears over the horizon. Use
   'because' as a joining word.

   _____

   _____

   _____

What Happens when Your Foot Goes to Sleep?

From your brain down your spine run motor and sensory nerves that are connected to all parts of your body. Motor nerves are connected to muscles, which are bands of flesh that move your legs or other parts of your body. Sensory nerves allow you to feel things. These nerves are linked to the brain like a telephone system.

Sometimes, when you sit in a chair so that a sharp edge presses the nerves of your leg, you may find that your foot has gone to sleep. What we mean by this is that you cannot move your foot or feel anything with it.

What has happened is that the pressure has affected the nerves serving your foot. By compressing the nerve fibres, it has made them incapable of transmitting impulses. If you attempt to rise and walk you cannot feel your foot because the sensory nerve has been pressed. You cannot direct the foot to act because the motor nerve too has been pressed. Your foot is numb.

Gradually the nerves recover as the pressure is removed, and you feel a tingling feeling which we call 'pins and needles' as the power returns.

1 Do sensory nerves help you feel things? _____

2 Are all your nerves connected to your brain? _____

3 If your foot is numb, and you cannot move it, which
   nerve besides the sensory nerve is affected? _____

4 What sort of a feeling is 'pins and needles'? _____

5 What are 'bands of flesh'? _____

6 Which word means 'pressing closely together'? _____

7 Which word means 'unable to feel or move'? _____

8 Which word means 'passing from one to another'? _____

9 Write the phrase in the second paragraph that tells where you sit.

   _____

10 From the first sentence in the second paragraph
   write the adjective. _____

11 When two adjectives are used to describe a noun, put a comma after the
   first one. Use the words below. Begin with the one written with a capital
   and put 'small' before 'sharp'. Put in the comma.

   nerves you any small feel Sensory bite sharp help

   _____

   _____

12 Write a sentence telling how a part of your body once became numb.

   _____

   _____

What Is Paper Made of?

Paper has been made of many kinds of plant material. Over the years cotton, clover, thistle, grass and all kinds of stalks have been made into paper. The Egyptians first made paper from the papyrus reed that grew along the banks of the Nile. For many centuries paper was made from old rags.

Today, paper is usually made from wood. Trees are cut down, the bark stripped from the trunks and the wood broken up into chips. The chips are cooked in chemicals to make wood pulp. The wood pulp enters a special machine that flattens it and turns it into paper. The machine is sometimes 90 metres long. The paper is rolled and squeezed as it moves along. At the end of the machine the paper is dried and then pressed to give it a smooth surface.

There are many different kinds of paper. Newsprint on which papers are printed is not as white and thick as other paper, and is cheaper to make. Paper for tissues or towelling has a lot of pulp made from rags.

Paper is now being used over and over again. We call this recycling. Don't throw paper in rubbish bins. Put it out for recycling. This will save many trees from being cut down.

COPIABLE PAGE   Key Curriculum Publications Ltd.

1   Has grass ever been used to make paper? _____

2   Is most of today's paper made from trees? _____

3   What has to be added to the water for the
cooking of wood chips? _____

4   What special name is given to the using of
paper over and over again? _____

5   Which word means 'hundreds of years'? _____

6   From what sort of reed was paper first made? _____

7   What sort of paper is used to make newspapers? _____

8   To make tissue paper and towelling,
what is used to make the pulp? _____

9   Write the adverbial phrase in the first sentence
of the second paragraph. _____

10 In the first sentence of the story, is the
word 'plant' a noun or an adjective? _____

11 Notice that commas follow a list of nouns in the second sentence. No
comma is used before a joining word. Write the sentence below putting in
the commas.

Paper can be thick thin plain or coloured.

_____

_____

12 Write a sentence about paper hats you saw at a party. Use three adjectives
together separated by two commas.

_____

_____

Why Do Our Faces Keep Warm without Clothes?

The way our body feels is a matter of what we are used to. Our faces, exposed to cold, do become cold, but they do not feel cold. This is because the nerves of the face, by which we feel cold, are used to this state of things. They take no notice.

People for thousands of years have walked around, and even gone to sleep wearing clothes, but have left their faces uncovered. On a winter's day we may not notice that our noses and ear-tips are cold. They are cold, though we do not feel cold. We only realise how cold our face is when we touch it with a warm hand.

You soon find that your feet become cold if you take off your shoes and socks on a cold day. But there are people who have never worn shoes and socks, so the nerves in their feet become used to being cold and they do not feel uncomfortable.

Some nerves in the body become used to changes very quickly. Country people often find it difficult to sleep in the city because of traffic noises. After a few nights the nerves of the ear and brain become accustomed to the noises and they sleep well. Of course, when they return to the country, their nerves must adjust to the quietness again.

1 Do our faces really become cold? _____

2 Are there people who have never worn shoes? _____

3 What part of the body gives us the
feeling of hot or cold? the _____

4 What sort of noises do we hear less in the country
than in the city? _____

5 Which word could be interchanged with 'used'? _____

6 Which word means 'uncovered or open to'? _____

7 Which word means 'understand fully'? _____

8 Which word means 'take off'? _____

9 The first sentence of the second paragraph has three parts. Write the two
joining words in the order they appear.

_____ _____

10 The last sentence has two pronouns—'they' and 'their'. These words stand
for the same adjective and a noun. Write them.

adjective _____ noun _____

11 Proofread the sentence below which has five mistakes. Write it correctly.

would a eskimo feal the cold less than you

_____

_____

12 Write a sentence beginning with 'When' about a time you felt really cold.

_____

_____

There are not more stars on some nights than on others, but we see more. What really occurs is that the state of the atmosphere, or space above us, is not always the same. Sometimes there are clouds in the sky which hide the stars. But even when there are no clouds, you may only be able to see the brightest stars.

The air above us may contain more dust than usual so that the less bright stars cannot be seen. Even the temperature where you are standing can have some effect on how well you see the stars.

In order to look at the stars, scientists use large telescopes built on top of mountains or in places where the air is not affected by smoke or dust. The higher the telescope, the less amount of air that the light from the stars has to pass through before it reaches the astronomer or the camera lens.

Two of the largest telescopes are at observatories in California, America. One is on Mount Wilson and the other on Mount Palomar. The Americans named them the 'Hale Observatories' after George E. Hale, who invented a special camera to film the Sun.

1 Can dust in the air prevent you seeing stars? _____

2 Are telescopes built in valleys between hills? _____

3 In which country is Mount Palomar? _____

4 Which star was filmed by Hale's camera? _____

5 Which word means 'happens'? _____

6 Which word means 'a mixture of gases that
   surrounds the Earth'? _____

7 Which word means 'a scientist who studies
   stars and planets'? _____

8 Which word means 'made up' or 'thought of'? _____

9 Look at the first sentence in the last paragraph.
   Write the adjective in its simplest form. _____

10 The third sentence in the first paragraph has
   two parts. Write the joining word. _____

11 Proofread the sentence below. Write it again correctly. There are words that
   need capitals. Insert one comma. The 'Sun' here is a proper noun, being the
   name of a star.

   scientists study the bright burning sun
   from mount palomar

   _____

   _____

12 Write a long sentence about a night when the sky was very clear as you
   looked at the stars. Begin with 'One night'.

   _____

   _____

What Are 'The Ashes'?

When the Australian cricket team came to England in 1882, they had a very strong side. Spofforth was the 'Demon Bowler' and Blackham was a superb wicket keeper.

There were only three test matches played. Both sides had won a test and the final one was being played to decide the rubber. After some exciting cricket, England were playing their last innings. They needed seven runs to win. They had one good batsman left, Studd, and a bowler who came in as the last man. The bowler, Peate, had only to block the ball and let Studd hit the runs.

Studd suddenly decided to swing at the ball and score a boundary. He was out! Australia had won. Afterwards, in a weekly sporting paper, a death notice was inserted:

"In affectionate remembrance of English Cricket, died on August 19, 1882. The body will be cremated and the Ashes taken to Australia."

The stumps used in the game were burned and the ashes were collected and placed in an urn. This urn is on display at the famous Lord's Cricket Ground in England. Ever since then, a series played between Australia and England is not called a 'rubber' but the 'Ashes'.

COPIABLE PAGE Key Curriculum Publications Ltd.

1 Was the score one all before the final rubber? _____

2 Did Australia win by seven runs? _____

3 What was the name of an English bowler? _____

4 Who was the Australian wicket keeper? _____

5 Which word means 'a person of great skill or energy'? _____

6 Which word means the same as 'show'? _____

7 Which word means 'a score of four or six at cricket'? _____

8 Which word means 'put in'? _____

9 Write the adjectives in the first sentence.

_____

10 Prepositions are little words that begin phrases. In the last paragraph the same three prepositions begin phrases. Write this little word. _____

11 Write the first sentence again, putting the conjunction 'when' in the middle.

_____

_____

12 Complete this sentence explaining where the 'Ashes' are kept. Your sentence must contain an adjective used in the story. Underline this adjective.

The Ashes _____

_____

What Is Artificial Silk?

We all probably know that silk is a strong, soft but expensive material spun from the threads made by silkworms. Long ago, the daughter of a Chinese Emperor found white caterpillars eating her father's mulberry trees. She unwound a thread from a cocoon and was the first to discover silk.

It is fun to keep the silkworm caterpillars, providing you have access to a mulberry tree, as these caterpillars feed on its leaves. You can then watch the silkworms spin cocoons which are made of silk.

In 1883, Sir Joseph Swan found a way of making silk artificially. Just as the silkworm caterpillar ejects fluid through spinnerets into the air which turn solid, so Sir Joseph squirted an emulsion of cellulose nitrate in acetic acid through minute holes into alcohol. The alcohol coagulated the emulsion into a thread. This thread was inflammable, so it had to be treated with ammonium sulphide to make it safe.

The process of making artificial silk has improved since it was first invented over a hundred years ago. Today, the silk thread can be made as fine as that of the silkworm and is much cheaper to produce.

Key Curriculum Publications Ltd.

1 Did a Chinese Emperor first unwind a cocoon
to discover silk thread? _____

2 Was artificial silk first made over 100 years ago? _____

3 On what kind of leaf does a silkworm feed? _____

4 What chemical hardened the emulsion to
make a thread solid? _____

5 Which word means 'a fine, milky fluid'? _____

6 Which word means 'throws out'? _____

7 which word means 'easily burnt'? _____

8 What do silkworms make when they spin silk? _____

9 Write the adverb in the first sentence. _____

10 Write the three adjectives from the same sentence.

_____ _____ _____

11 The last sentence in the first paragraph is written in the past tense. Write
the sentence again, changing the first two verbs so that they are in the
present tense (happening now).

_____

_____

12 Write the start of a conversation between the daughter and the Emperor
when she first tells him what she had discovered. Write the words he used in
reply. Use quotation marks around words actually spoken.

_____

_____

5　　*1* no *2* yes *3* worker *4* poison *5* provoked *6* prevents
7 withdrawing *8* yes *9* rarely *10* unless *11* Bees sometimes
sting painfully, but they always make honey. *12* parent or
teacher to correct.

7　　*1* yes *2* no *3* six *4* insects *5* two *6* vision *7* smaller
8 compound *9* because *10* directly, behind *11* Most insects
and ants have large compound eyes. *12* parent or teacher to
correct.

9　　*1* yes *2* no *3* creaking *4* frame *5* similar *6* smaller *7* cooler
8 house-breaker *9* question *10* heard, was *11* Have you
heard creaking in your house at night? *12* parent or teacher
to correct

11　　*1* no *2* no *3* yes *4* bone *5* decay *6* fresh *7* healing
8 darkness *9* never *10* but *11* I saw Helen break her arm
when she fell. *12* parent or teacher to correct.

13　　*1* no *2* star *3* Earth, Venus *4* star *5* reflects *6* orbits
7 distant *8* steady *9* glowing *10* brightly *11* Venus looks like
a <u>bright</u> star in the sky. *12* parent or teacher to correct.

15　　*1* yes *2* no *3* Guam *4* chasm *5* varies *6* apparatus
7 supersonic *8* time *9* sounding *10* Guam *11* Guam lies to
the east of the Philippine Islands. *12* parent or teacher to
correct.

17　　*1* no *2* no *3* play *4* aeroplane *5* resists *6* curved
7 permanently *8* outwards *9* in a circle *10* Australian
Aborigines *11* A boomerang can travel a distance of almost one
(or a) hundred metres before returning. *12* parent or teacher
to correct.

19　　*1* yes *2* no *3* plankton *4* lifesavers *5* search *6* tenth *7*
minute *8* crushing *9* huge *10* Australia, America, Japan *11*
You can swim <u>safely</u> between flags at the beach. *12* parent
or teacher to correct.

Key Curriculum Publications Ltd.

21   *1* no *2* no *3* oxygen *4* frozen *5* cold-blooded *6* surface *7* process
8 replenished *9* in a drink *10* on top *11* Yes, I have noticed that
ice cubes in a drink float on top. *12* parent or teacher to correct.

23   *1* no *2* no *3* short *4* accident *5* control *6* adults *7* occurs
8 worries, problems *9* out of bed *10* sleepwalker, bed *11* There
are two parts of the brain. *12* parent or teacher to correct.

25   *1* yes *2* no *3* gently *4* hurricane *5* trembling *6* draught *7* chinks
8 property *9* wind *10* during a hurricane *11* A yacht needs the
wind to make it move. *12* parent or teacher to correct.

27   *1* sailors *2* yes *3* no *4* architects *5* gigantic, giant *6* calm
7 foundations *8* describe *9* triangular *10* tall *11* When it was
used, they were in calm seas. *12* parent or teacher to correct.

29   *1* liquid *2* no *3* hot *4* gas *5* continually *6* deposited *7* touches
8 Sweden *9* very *10* it *11* Water in the air of a room is there,
although you cannot see it. *12* parent or teacher to correct.

31   *1* yes *2* coal *3* electric *4* yes *5* exhaust, fumes *6* pollution
7 imperfect *8* speaks *9* Australia, England *10* and, which
11 If most things were burnt properly, they would give off little
or no smoke. *12* parent or teacher to correct.

33   *1* yes *2* no *3* curved *4* ships *5* centre *6* melted *7* law
8 approach *9* rubber *10* gradually *11* a liquid always finds
its own level. *12* parent or teacher to correct.

35   *1* yes *2* yes *3* motor *4* tingling *5* muscles *6* compressing
7 numb *8* transmitting *9* in a chair *10* sharp *11* Sensory nerves
help you feel any small, sharp bite. *12* parent or teacher to correct

37   *1* yes *2* yes *3* chemical *4* recycling *5* centuries *6* papyrus
7 newsprint *8* rags *9* from wood *10* adjective *11* Paper can be
thick, thin, plain or coloured. *12* parent or teacher to correct.

Answers

39 *1* yes *2* yes *3* nerves *4* traffic *5* accustomed *6* exposed *7* realise *8* remove *9* and, but *10* country people *11* Would an Eskimo feel the cold less than you? *12* parent or teacher to correct.

41 *1* yes *2* no *3* America *4* Sun *5* occurs *6* atmosphere *7* astronomer *8* invented *9* large *10* which *11* Scientists study the bright, burning Sun from Mount Palomar. *12* parent or teacher to correct.

43 *1* yes *2* no *3* Peate *4* Blackham *5* demon *6* display *7* boundary *8* inserted *9* Australian, cricket, strong *10* in *11* The Australian cricket team had a very strong side when they came to England in 1882. *12* parent or teacher to correct.

45 *1* no *2* yes *3* mulberry *4* alcohol *5* emulsion *6* ejects *7* inflammable *8* cocoons *9* probably *10* strong, soft, expensive *11* She unwinds the thread from a cocoon and is the first to discover silk. *12* parent or teacher to correct.

Key Curriculum Publications Ltd.